THE LITERARY GUILD®
READER'S JOURNAL

THE LITERARY GUILD®

READER'S JOURNAL

BOOKSPAN
Garden City, New York

Opening passages reprinted from:

Evergreen by Belva Plain, published by Delacorte Press
The Naked and the Dead by Norman Mailer, published by Henry Holt and Company
The Good Earth by Pearl S. Buck, published by Simon and Schuster, Inc.
Forever Amber by Kathleen Winsor, published by The Macmillan Company
Big Stone Gap by Adriana Trigiani, published by Random House
Rebecca by Daphne du Maurier, published by Doubleday and Company, Inc.
The Bean Trees by Barbara Kingsolver, published by HarperCollins Publishers, Inc.
Roots by Alex Haley, published by Doubleday and Company, Inc.
Saratoga Trunk by Edna Ferber, published by Doubleday, Doran and Company, Inc.
Where the Heart Is by Billie Letts, published by Warner Books
To Love Again by Danielle Steel, published by Dell Publishing Company, Inc.
To Kill a Mockingbird by Harper Lee, published by HarperCollins Publishers, Inc.
Winnie-the-Pooh by A.A. Milne, published by E.P. Dutton and Company, Inc.
Scruples by Judith Krantz, published by Crown Publishers, Inc.
Harry Potter and the Chamber of Secrets by J.K. Rowling, published by Scholastic Inc.

GRAND OPENINGS

"In the beginning there was a warm room with a table, a black iron stove and old red-flowered wallpaper."
—*Evergreen* by Belva Plain

_____

_____

_____

_____

_____

_____

_____

_____

_____

_____

_____

_____

_____

_____

My Favorite Books by Belva Plain

1. *David Copperfield* by Charles Dickens

2. *The Fortunes of Richard Mahoney* by Henry H. Richardson

3. *Kristin Lavransdatter* by Sigrid Undset

4. *Tess of the D'Urbervilles* by Thomas Hardy

5. *Buddenbrooks* by Thomas Mann

TRISTAM

by Edward Arlington Robinson was a MAIN SELECTION in 1927. This Arthurian work won the 1928 Pulitzer Prize.

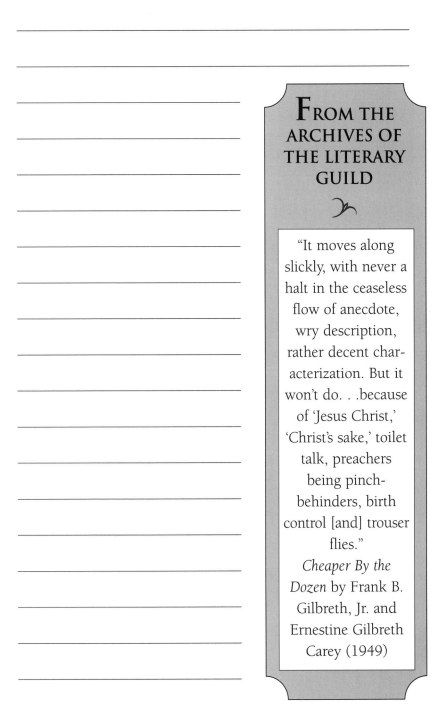

THE LAST POET

by Ford Madox Ford was a MAIN SELECTION in 1928.
This book is still available in book stores—in its Literary
Guild edition!

" 'Christmas won't be Christmas without any presents,'
grumbled Jo, lying on the rug."
—*Little Women* by Louisa May Alcott

"Nobody could sleep. When morning came, assault craft would be lowered and a first wave of troops would ride through the surf and charge ashore on the beach at Anopopei."
—*The Naked and the Dead* by Norman Mailer

_____

_____

_____

_____

_____

_____

_____

_____

_____

_____

_____

_____

_____

_____

MAMBA'S DAUGHTERS

by Du Bose Heyward was a MAIN SELECTION in 1929.
Heyward also wrote the book, *Porgy*, that inspired the
George and Ira Gershwin opera, *Porgy and Bess*.

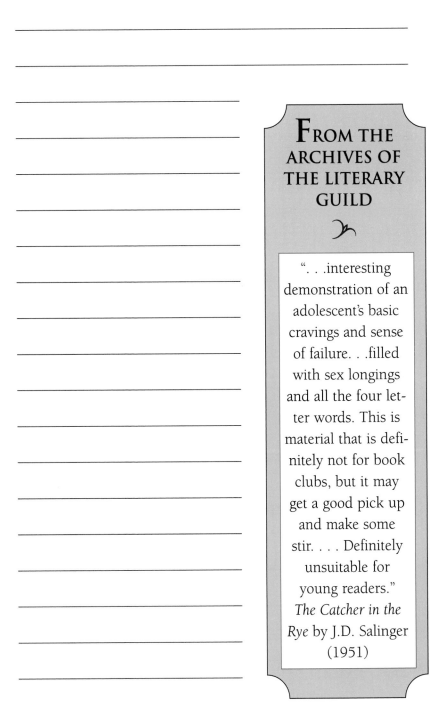

THE GREAT MEADOW

by Elizabeth Madox Roberts was a MAIN SELECTION in 1930. It's one of the author's many novels about Kentucky, where she was born in 1886.

MY FAVORITE AUTHORS BY SUE GRAFTON

1. Anthony Trollope

2. Jane Austen

3. Anne Lamott

4. Mary Karr

5. Elmore Leonard

$\mathcal{M}$Y FAVORITE MYSTERIES BY SUE GRAFTON

1. *Beyond a Reasonable Doubt* by C.W. Grafton

2. *Cat Chaser* by Elmore Leonard

3. *The Speed Queen* by Stewart O'Nan

4. *The High Window* by Raymond Chandler

5. *Double Indemnity* by James M. Cain

JOHN HENRY

by Roark Bradford was a MAIN SELECTION in 1931. Bradford wrote primarily about African-Americans. His works include the novel that was the basis of the play, *The Green Pastures*.

_____

_____

_____

_____

_____

_____

_____

_____

_____

_____

_____

_____

_____

_____

_____

_____

_____

GRAND OPENINGS

"It was Wang Lung's marriage day."
—*The Good Earth* by Pearl S. Buck

_____

_____

_____

_____

_____

_____

_____

_____

_____

_____

_____

_____

_____

_____

_____

_____

STATE FAIR

by Philip Stong was a MAIN SELECTION in 1932. This heartland story holds the honor of being made into a movie not once, but three times: in 1933 starring Will Rogers, in 1945 starring Dana Andrews and in 1962 starring Pat Boone.

THE AUTOBIOGRAPHY OF ALICE B. TOKLAS

by Gertrude Stein was a MAIN SELECTION in 1933. This famous expatriate author earned an M.D. degree from Johns Hopkins Medical School.

GRAND OPENINGS

"The small room was warm and moist. Furious blasts of thunder made the window-panes rattle and lightning seemed to streak through the room itself."
—*Forever Amber* by Kathleen Winsor

_____

_____

_____

_____

_____

_____

_____

_____

_____

_____

_____

_____

_____

PERSONAL HISTORY

by Vincent Sheean was a MAIN SELECTION in 1935. Sheean worked as a foreign correspondent. This best-selling memoir opened America's eyes to Europe's coming storm.

_____

_____

_____

_____

_____

_____

_____

_____

_____

_____

_____

_____

_____

${\mathcal{M}}$Y FAVORITE BOOKS BY JACKIE COLLINS

1. *The Great Gatsby* by F. Scott Fitzgerald—a wonderful read, and a classic that I try to re-read once a year.

2. *The Godfather* by Mario Puzo—one of the great storytellers of all time.

3. *The Carpetbaggers* by Harold Robbins—who started the whole blockbuster syndrome and was also a great storyteller.

4. Anything by Dickens—the master!

GRAND OPENINGS

"This will be a good weekend for reading."
—*Big Stone Gap* by Adriana Trigiani

ONE LIFE, ONE KOPEK

by Walter Duranty was a MAIN SELECTION in 1937.
Duranty was a famous foreign correspondent. This was
his first novel.

My favorite authors by James Patterson

1. Kent Anderson

2. Elmore Leonard

3. Walter Mosley

4. Dennis Lehane

5. Stephen King

6. Nelson DeMille

REBECCA

by Daphne du Maurier was a MAIN SELECTION in 1938.
This legendary tale of romantic suspense was turned into
one of the many thrilling films of Alfred Hitchcock, starring
Joan Fontaine and Laurence Olivier.

GRAND OPENINGS

"Last night I dreamt I went to Manderley again."
—*Rebecca* by Daphne du Maurier

_____

_____

_____

_____

_____

_____

_____

_____

_____

_____

_____

_____

_____

_____

My favorite books by Anne River Siddons

1. *One Hundred Years of Solitude* by Gabriel Garcia Marquez

2. *A Good Scent from a Strange Mountain* by Robert Olen Butler

3. *Mariette in Ecstasy* by Ron Hansen

4. *The Once and Future King* by T.H. White

My favorite authors by Anne River Siddons

1. Henry James

2. Edith Wharton

3. Walker Percy

4. Herman Melville

5. Pat Conroy

CHRISTMAS HOLIDAY

by W. Somerset Maugham was a MAIN SELECTION in 1939.
A prolific author for Doubleday, Maugham wrote the classic
Of Human Bondage.

"I have been afraid of putting air in a tire ever since I saw a tractor tire blow up and throw Newt Hardbine's father over the top of the Standard Oil sign."
—*The Bean Trees* by Barbara Kingsolver

_____

_____

_____

_____

_____

_____

_____

_____

_____

_____

_____

_____

_____

WORLD'S END

by Upton Sinclair was a MAIN SELECTION in 1940. This is
the first novel in Sinclair's *Lanny Budd* series. A social
activist, Sinclair also wrote the classic *The Jungle*.

GRAND OPENINGS

"Early in the spring of 1750, in the village of Juffure, four days upriver from the coast of The Gambia, West Africa, a manchild was born to Omoro and Binta Kinte."
—*Roots* by Alex Haley

_____

_____

_____

_____

_____

_____

_____

_____

_____

_____

_____

_____

_____

_____

_____

A TREE GROWS IN BROOKLYN

by Betty Smith was a MAIN SELECTION in 1943. This heartbreaking coming-of-age novel was made into a classic film, the first directed by Elia Kazan.

GRAND OPENINGS

"Dorothy lived in the midst of the great Kansas prairies,
with Uncle Henry, who was a farmer, and Aunt Em,
who was the farmer's wife."
—*The Wonderful Wizard of Oz* by L. Frank Baum

_____

_____

_____

_____

_____

_____

_____

_____

_____

_____

_____

_____

_____

GREAT SON

by Edna Ferber was a MAIN SELECTION in 1945. A frequent Selection author, Ferber also wrote *Show Boat*, *So Big* and *Giant*.

GRAND OPENINGS

"They were interviewing Clint Maroon. They were always interviewing old Colonel Maroon."
—*Saratoga Trunk* by Edna Ferber

My Favorite Books by Anna Quindlen

1. *Main Street* by Sinclair Lewis

2. *My Antonia* by Willa Cather

3. *The Lion, the Witch, and the Wardrobe* by C.S. Lewis

4. *Wuthering Heights* by Emily Brontë

5. *Jane Eyre* by Charlotte Brontë

6. *The Group* by Mary McCarthy

7. *The Blue Swallows* by Howard Nemerov (poetry)

8. *The Phantom Tollbooth* by Norton Juster

9. *A Christmas Carol* by Charles Dickens

10. *Scoop* by Evelyn Waugh

"There was no possibility of taking a walk that day."
—*Jane Eyre* by Charlotte Brontë

_____

_____

_____

_____

_____

_____

_____

_____

_____

_____

_____

_____

_____

_____

THE AMERICAN

by Howard Fast was a MAIN SELECTION in 1946. Fast was still writing popular fiction at the turn of the twentieth century. As 1999 came to a close, he published *Redemption*, a novel of suspense.

_____

_____

_____

_____

_____

_____

_____

_____

_____

_____

_____

_____

_____

_____

_____

_____

MY FAVORITE BOOKS BY SUSAN ISAACS

1. *Pride and Prejudice* by Jane Austen

2. *Jane Eyre* by Charlotte Brontë

3. *I Capture the Castle* by Dodie Smith

4. *Great Expectations* by Charles Dickens

"My father's family name being Pirrip, and my Christian name Phillip, my infant tongue could make of both names nothing longer or more explicit than Pip."
—*Great Expectations* by Charles Dickens

I CAPTURE THE CASTLE

by Dodie Smith was a MAIN SELECTION in 1948. Dodie Smith is also the author of *101 Dalmations*.

My Favorite Authors by Eric Jerome Dickey

1. Stephen King

2. Sue Grafton

3. Walter Mosley

4. Colin Harrison

5. James Patterson

6. Lolita Files

7. Kimberla Roby

8. E. Lynn Harris

REST AND BE THANKFUL

by Helen MacInness was a MAIN SELECTION in 1949. Helen MacInnes wrote espionage bestsellers as recently as 1989.

MY FAVORITE BOOKS BY EILEEN GOUDGE

1. *Green Dolphin Street by* Elizabeth Goudge

2. *The Stand* by Stephen King

3. *The War Between the Tates* by Alison Lurie

4. *Three Women at the Water's Edge* by Nancy Thayer

5. *Animal Dreams* by Barbara Kingsolver

GRAND OPENINGS

"Novalee Nation, seventeen, seven months pregnant, thirty-seven pounds overweight—and superstitious about sevens—shifted uncomfortably in the seat of the old Plymouth and ran her hands down the curve of her belly."
—*Where the Heart Is* by Billie Letts

_____

_____

_____

_____

_____

_____

_____

_____

_____

_____

_____

_____

_____

_____

MY COUSIN RACHEL

by Daphne du Maurier was a MAIN SELECTION in 1952.
This bestseller by the author of *Rebecca* was made into
a 1953 movie starring Richard Burton and Olivia
de Havilland.

BEYOND THIS PLACE

by A.J. Cronin was a MAIN SELECTION in 1953. Cronin was a Scottish doctor who wrote several works that became Literary Guild Main Selections.

THE MAN IN THE GRAY FLANNEL SUIT

by Sloan Wilson was a MAIN SELECTION in 1955. Wilson's take on the professional rat race, this novel became a hit movie starring Gregory Peck.

GRAND OPENINGS

"In every city there is a time of year that approaches perfection."
—*To Love Again* by Danielle Steel

TO KILL A MOCKINGBIRD

by Harper Lee was a MAIN SELECTION in 1960. This novel is a beloved bestseller to this day. Gregory Peck won the Oscar® for Best Actor for his portrayal of Atticus Finch in the acclaimed film.

MY FAVORITE BOOKS BY HOMER HICKAM

1. *Treasure Island* by Robert Louis Stevenson

2. *Cannery Row* by John Steinbeck

3. *Huckleberry Finn* by Mark Twain

4. *Master and Commander* by Patrick O'Brian

5. *Principles of Guided Missile Design* by Bonney, Zucrow, and Besserer

6. *The Iliad* by Homer

7. *To Kill a Mockingbird* by Harper Lee

8. *Starship Troopers* by Robert Heinlein

"When he was nearly thirteen, my brother Jem got his arm badly broken at the elbow."
—*To Kill a Mockingbird* by Harper Lee

_____

_____

_____

_____

_____

_____

_____

_____

_____

_____

_____

_____

_____

_____

_____

WYOMING SUMMER

by Mary O'Hara was a MAIN SELECTION in 1963. O'Hara's
works include the classics, *My Friend Flicka* and
Thunderhead.

GRAND OPENINGS

"Here is Edward Bear, coming downstairs now, bump, bump, bump, on the back of his head, behind Christopher Robin."
—*Winnie-the-Pooh* by A.A. Milne

THE LOOKING GLASS

by John LeCarré was a MAIN SELECTION in 1965. LeCarre's body of work includes *The Spy Who Came in From the Cold* which, on its 1963 publication, was called by Graham Greene the "finest spy story ever written."

_____

_____

_____

_____

_____

_____

_____

_____

_____

_____

_____

_____

_____

_____

WHEN SHE WAS GOOD

by Philip Roth was a MAIN SELECTION in 1953. Roth won America's four top literary prizes with four books in the 1990s: *Patrimony*, National Book Critics Circle Award (1991); *Operation Shylock*, PEN/Faulkner Award (1993); *Sabbath's Theater*, National Book Award (1995); *American Pastoral*, Pulitzer Prize (1998).

MY FAVORITE BOOKS BY JOY FIELDING

1. *The Human Stain* by Philip Roth

2. *American Pastoral* by Philip Roth

3. *The Hours* by Michael Cunningham

4. *Tourist Season* by Carl Hiaasen

5. *The Prince of Tides* by Pat Conroy

6. *Play it as it Lays* by Joan Didion

SERPICO

by Peter Maas was a MAIN SELECTION in 1973. The Literary Guild's tradition of selling real-life drama stretches from Eve Curie's biography of her mother, Marie Curie, in 1937, to Frank McCourt's memoir of coming to America, '*Tis*, in 1999.

"In Beverly Hills only the infirm and the senile do not drive their own cars."
—*Scruples* by Judith Krantz

THE SECOND STAGE

by Betty Friedan was a MAIN SELECTION in 1982. This new blueprint for living was published twenty years after Friedan's *The Feminine Mystique*, which helped trigger one of the most powerful social movements of our time.

My Favorite Books by Barbara Delinsky

1. *The Scarlet Letter* by Nathaniel Hawthorne

2. *A Tale of Two Cities* by Charles Dickens

3. *The Awakening* by Kate Chopin

4. *The Old Man and the Sea* by Ernest Hemingway

5. Anything *Harry Potter* by J.K. Rowling

"Not for the first time, an argument had broken out over breakfast at number four, Privet Drive."
—*Harry Potter and the Chamber of Secrets* by J.K. Rowling